LETTIE MURII

Her L

1880-

Compiled by

James C. A. Burnett of Leys

Leys Publishing

Banchory Business Centre, Burn O'Bennie Road,

Banchory, Aberdeenshire, AB31 5ZU

A monstrous grandfather with a loathing for Roman Catholicism.

A father, who suffered under his father, forbidden to be a Catholic until on his deathbed, which in turn allowed the estate of this lower noble Scottish family to fall to its knees.

A teenage daughter chose to commit to the service of God, determined to become a Catholic despite family opposition. With her brothers, she brought the family back to be amongst the most celebrated, and herself became a legend in her own time.

That daughter was Lettie.

Contents

Illustrations

Preface

Accepting that my views are biased, it did not take me long to become in love with Lettie. Whether it was affectionate or familial, playful or obsessive, or just the admiration of the selfless love of Lettie herself, I do not know. Maybe a bit of each.

This is not a biography. It is a compilation of letters of Lettie Muriel Burnett. There are selections from her illustrated writings as a teenager to her younger sister, the thoughts of a protector of her young charges in the Tsar's circle in St Petersburg and of her family back in Scotland, and some of a mother to her girls as the much loved and hugely respected Mistress General at the Convent of the Sacred Heart at Roehampton.

The letters are not numerous, but there is no better way of understanding the nature and character of a lady who gave her life wholly for the benefit of others. Her access to the Lord above is reflected in her benevolence. There are times when she appears to be a little severe, but any severity was undoubtedly linked to her kindness and therefore in the interest of her charges. She was serious, but also humorous, and maybe occasionally a little wicked, albeit to a degree insufficient to deny her a special relationship with God.

We need to look a little further than to the lives of her grandfather and her father to understand one reason for her desire to be a Catholic,. For that reason, I have included some detail of past generations in the following chapter.

Lettie's own memoirs are retained in the Convent's archive. It was researched by her niece, Susan Burnett of Kemnay, for her family history, *Without Fanfare*, from which I have drawn some detail and particularly something of her forebears. Lettie's life at the Convent is also well summarised in the eulogy provided by Mary Don, another Sacred Heart pupil, who was also fortunate enough to have been well acquainted with Lettie.

Kemnay

I became aware of Lettie when creating a presentation of the Burnetts of Kemnay in the Family Room at my home, Crathes Castle, near Aberdeen, where there are displays of Burnett connections and particularly of the more celebrated. The Burnetts of Kemnay may not be the closest of cousins because the branch grew out in about 1600. Regardless, in addition to friendship, consanguinity and geographical proximity, the degree of celebrity and respect encourages us to count them as nearer relations than genealogical charts suggest.

I soon realised that Lettie was a very special person, and a very special Burnett. Reading her letters creates more than mere empathy. The early illustrated ones to her younger sister may encourage the reader to follow her progress through life. They may also provide some letter-writing inspiration to today's younger generation.

The correspondence relating to Lettie's younger days at school and at Tsarskoe Selo have been given to me by her cousins, the late Mhairi Bogdan and her son Robbie Bogdan, formerly of Barra Castle in Aberdeenshire.

Barra by James Giles

Where it relates to her reign as Mistress General at the Convent of the Sacred Heart at Roehampton, I am grateful to Alice Shields whose mother had the good fortune to be a pupil of Mother Burnett.

The gift to the Burnett archive of letters relating to Lettie's life prompted me to record some of her correspondence for the benefit of others. If this includes material which may not appear to be of particular interest, it is because I considered it wrong for this account not to be a reasonably comprehensive record and because the letters are not stored in the same location, they are unlikely to be viewed together. It is also a good way to understand the mind of this special person. Her early commitment of dedication to Roman Catholicism, despite strong parental opposition, says much.

My vision of Lettie stems from the letters and a modicum of research. Lettie may well have had a darker side of which we are unaware, but I have assumed that is not so from what I have heard and read.

Canonization may be required to be supported by evidence of miracles. I accept that my view of Lettie may be a little biased, but in my opinion, it might also be considered for the earthly actions of a human being who just gave everything in the interest of others. Others may not agree and I may misunderstand the qualifications required to become a Saint. If not, Lettie would prove to be an admirable candidate. Such a nomination would surely have been supported by Madeleine Sophie Barat, the founder of the Convent in 1800 and who eventually received that honour.

James Burnett of Leys

The Burnetts of Kemnay

There are a few family members whose names appear in the letters. Here is a selection of Lettie's closest relations with some brief descriptive notes. Any assessment of Lettie must take into account the family into which she was born and their attitude towards her beliefs.

To understand the formality of her letters, we have to frame her not only in the context of the times, but also with the nature of some of the older members of her family.

1) Alexander Burnett 1816 – 1908, 6th Laird of Kemnay. By all accounts, he was not a nice man. One of his daughters said she was sure that he never knew her name as he never referred to her as anything else but "Child." The things he liked best were his food and writing to the papers.

He had a small dog which he quite liked and he used to ring the outside bell at the back door if the animal was missing at mealtimes and the dog would come running back from the village for his dinner. He showed more affection for the dog that he ever did for his children.

Roman Catholicism was his prime hate and he wrote lengthy condemnations so extreme and malicious that it is a wonder he was never taken to court. Some of his essays or sermons which he wrote were just the rantings of a sanctimonious bigot and he was probably never taken seriously. In secular affairs he was tyrannical and contentious, and from the muniments in the archive, one finds numerous accounts of interdicts and court cases against his tenants or local merchants.

He let Kemnay fall into a very poor condition, leased it and went to the Continent. To finance his travels and his children's welfare, he sold off sites in the village.

His first wife died a few days after the birth of their daughter Amy. The life of a celibate held no charms for Alexander and he remarried. His second wife died not long after the birth of their daughter Frances. He styled himself the Reverend and preached a sermon in Kemnay chapel "Christianity - an antidote to weeping" on the occasion of his wife's death.

In 1893 he married again for a third time. Emily was a kind caring woman and showed her little stepdaughter, Frances, the only love she could remember receiving. Alexander and Emily died in 1908

His 10 children included:

a) John Burnett 1852 – 1935. 7th Laird of Kemnay

b) Amelia 1855 – 1941. Amy appointed herself the chatelaine and ruled the roost at Kemnay before and after her father's death and regardless of her stepmother. She was good to the estate tenants, but she was very strict with her stepsisters and particularly Frances whom she refused to allow to go to school. She was made to continue living with Amy at the Braes of Bennachie even after Amy was married to the Reverend James Stark - because she was useful.

c) Frances (Francie) 1884 – 1976. - see Amelia above. She was never able to stick up for herself when Amy treated her unkindly which she did to a greater extent as she became older. Amy's last words to her when Francie was dying were, "I hate you Francie, you are a fool."

2) John Burnett 1852 – 1935. 7th Laird of Kemnay. He married Charlotte Susan Forbes Gordon of Rayne. 10 Chanonry, was her Aberdeen home. He qualified in law and medicine and was a brilliant sportsman. He played cricket for Surrey and captained the Scottish Curling team. Despite a modicum of training, he was a hopeless businessman and took the Kemnay estate to the brink of financial ruin. His father had held the view that it was it was hardly worth educating him for a profession because he would inherit the estate and there was no need to learn anything about that. He was not allowed to join the army and did not inherit the Kemnay estate until he was 56 by which time he had borrowed heavily.

He became a friend of Richard D'Oyly Carte and accepted the post of 'Medic' with the opera company.

He travelled with the company touring American cities in 1882, staging Gilbert and Sullivan operas. There is no record of what he was paid by the company, but money continued to be a problem. However, he remained a lifelong friend of the D'Oyly Carte company who made a number of visits to Aberdeen. There was also another relation, Percy Anderson, who worked for D'Oyly Carte as a designer and so there was no surprise that the next generation were brought upon Gilbert and Sullivan.

When war broke out in 1914, he tried to enlist, but was turned down because of his age. Determined to serve in some way, he enlisted with the French Ambulance Corps until he was gassed and later awarded the Croix de Guerre.

He never said a horrid word about his father. But there are a few remaining letters to suggest the opposite.

Regardless of his father's aversion, his wife's parents refused to allow their daughter to marry a Catholic. John became a Roman Catholic on his death bed in the presence of his daughter, Lettie.

John and Charlotte's children included:

i)   Arthur 8th Laird 1878 – 1948. He was a prominent Freemason and had a jute broking business. A man held in the greatest esteem despite being publicly less prominent than his brothers

ii) Lettie Muriel 1880 - 1966

Lettie Muriel

iii) Charles 1882 -1945. Air Chief Marshall (Doodie) so named because he was born in the USA, (Yankee Doodle), while his parents were touring with D'Oyly Carte.

He had a distinguished career in the Air Force and was responsible for the training and excellence of the pilots who helped to win the Battle of Britain. He married Sybil, (known as Aunt Bowf), who was previously the wife of his commanding officer.

iv) Thomas (Tom) MBE 1885 – 1940. He had a notable and successful career in the Fleet Air Arm

v) Robert (Robin) 1887 – 1948. Admiral and Commander in Chief of the South Atlantic Fleet. 'Bob Burnett of the Barents Sea' commanded the operation that sunk the Scharnhorst. He was married to Connie.

vi) Irene Dorothy 1893 – 1982. Married Quentin Irvine of Barra and Straloch.

Dorothy's children included:

Mary Mhairi Irvine b.1916. Married Dr Andrew Bogdan(ovitch). Their children included Robbie Bogdan.

Early days

Lettie Muriel Burnett was born in June 1880, second child of John Burnett of Kemnay and his wife, Charlotte Forbes. Lettie, or Letty as she was to some of the family and at one time described by herself, was one of six children. Dorothy, one of the six, was the recipient of some of the correspondence below.

Her parents went to America with the D'Oyly Carte Opera in 1882 and Lettie was left in the care of her maternal grandmother at No 10 Chanonry, Aberdeen and with whom she spent most of her early days.

10 Chanonry Aberdeen

Lettie wrote in her memoirs that she adored her Grandmother, who, with a devoted Nanny, filled her Mother's place during the first ten years of her life. 'No child could have been happier - but I'm afraid that I was spoilt!' She remembered only two visits from her parents during the first eight years, each time made exciting by the appearance of a new brother.

Her Mother returned from America when she was ten and she spent a riotous holiday trying to do everything the brothers did, after which her Mother decided she could manage boys but not girls, and Lettie was sent back to her Grandmother in Edinburgh. She then had a German governess whom she hated, and who taught her nothing until she discovered the poor woman was devoted to cats, after which she reversed her opinion!

In her memoir she wrote "In 1890 I was in Princes Street with my nurse. At the far end was a gypsy with budgerigars who offered to tell fortunes. On the tray were some tiny coloured envelopes, and the bird, when taken from the cage, would pick out one with its beak. My nurse let me ask for one. I read what was inside but would not let my nurse see it, but, as I dropped the envelope, she picked it up and read 'You will enter a Convent'. The only thing I knew about Convents was from Sir Walter Scott's book *The Monastery* where I think, a nun is walled up!"

It could not have been a pleasant thought for a ten-year-old! But the sequel is the strange part.

"Ten years later when I was just twenty, walking with the same old nurse, we met another gypsy woman who offered to tell my fortune. She took my hand in hers and said, 'I see Convent written across.' I told her that I had never been in one. 'Nevertheless, I see Convent written across' was all she would say."

Growing up

In 1898 when her family moved to England, Lettie was sent to a boarding school at Eastbourne which she hated. It was only the thought that her brothers would say it was cowardice that kept her from running away. However, she much enjoyed the eighteen months she had spent at a school in Switzerland.

Her early letters to her sister, Dorothy, who was thirteen years her junior, are worthy of inclusion. They not only demonstrate her devotion to her sister, but also patience, originality and artistic skills which she clearly possessed.

1898 to her sister Dorothy from a Swiss Finishing School in Neuchatel. Dorothy was just 5 years old at the time.

Montmirail

Neuchâtel d

Suisse

day 17th. Feb. 1898.

My est Coz. Sies

am
awfully sorry to h'
from mummy that
you are (this bed
does not look very
comfortable, doesn't?)
How is your darling
little it is such a
pet; do you remember
the drive I had with
my nice Miss Ferguson

who has just been
married; how fast
the poney went.
faster than
their carraige
with the two horses!!
Every
three
weeks
we have a "soirée" and
the girls recite and
play the piano.
had to
recite a piece of
poetry last wednesday
I 'am glad that is over!!
& when we go into

the salle-à-manger.
each room devides (there
are 3) and go to their
own tables. I am in

Ch. 3. so of
course go
to the 3rd table
A. is the gouvernesse's table (E)
B. is monsieur Richels chair
D. is the chair for the girl
who recites (not to sit on! but to
stand behind!) C. is the
piano. H. is the head girls
Table. when the soirée is
finished the piano is
taken away, and the
tables A & H joined ! I

16

hope you will be able to understand ˮ! Each room has 2 "gones". and about 14 girls, there are 12 head girls (who think themselves awfully grand.) from the garden we can see the alps.

which even in the hottest time of summer are white with snow. now dear Coz. I have to stop, as here is the end of my paper and time. Goodbye very much love from Pettie W. Brunell.

On rejoining her mother, she met and made friends with a Roman Catholic family in Aberdeen, the Hays of Seaton. It was Miss Hay who took her to the Convent of the Sacred Heart at Queen's Cross and introduced her to the Reverend Mother Walpole who was to become her great friend and counsellor. There were many questions in her mind, and she eventually plucked up the courage to speak to her mother about her wish to convert to Roman Catholicism. Her wish was opposed with the suggestion of a year's moratorium on the subject. The day on which the year was finished, Lettie presented herself to the Convent for instruction.

Lettie became a Roman Catholic in December 1903.

The next few years were spent travelling the Continent and visiting friends, but always keeping in touch with Mother Walpole. From quite an early age Lettie could draw beautifully and many of her letters to Dorothy, who would have been 10 years old, are delightfully illustrated. Some of her letters were written from their home at 10 The Chanonry in Old Aberdeen when Dorothy was ill with measles.

10 Chanonry
Old Aberdeen.

my dear Dorothy

. . I expect you are
feeling a good bit
better again. It was rather
hard that you should have
the misssssssels worse than
me, was'nt it? You see how
sorry I am for you at
the top of the page. I am
going to draw you a picture
of the measle microbe.
no wonder
people are
frightened at
it. You have   often

heard people say they are
afraid they will catch
the measles; it is not
they who catch the measles
they could'nt if they
tried; It is the measles
that catch them.

what can you do against
a microbe with <u>ten</u> legs!
The way I caught. I

mean the way the measles
caught me, was this _ (mind
you do'nt tell anyone.)
I was coming home one
afternoon when I heard
a sort of coughing noise
and looking round I saw
a regiment of measle
microbes after me; I took
to my heals and ran,
and you know I can
run fast though I am
fat! but it was
no good, before I
could turn up the avenue
they caught me. so do'nt

try and run away from a measle microbe, it's no good –

This is the sad little micobe that Dr Edmond sent home again.

Goodbye – Lettie

Miss D. Burnett

Why don't we illustrate our letters like this today? It might encourage more young people to take up art. Lettie should be admired for her imagination and patience and her concern for her little sister.

The next one is also to Dorothy who, as a ten-year-old, would have been expected to recognise Bible scenes.

☀day.   10 Chanonry
                          Old Aberdeen.
                                  4ʰ Feb. 1903

My dear Dorothy.

    As this is Sunday I
will give you some Bible pictures
to guess instead of microbes!
The first one
is very easy
I expect you
will guess it
at once.

Do'nt you think the second is
a fine one? I am afraid I
am makeing them too easy.

24

III

IV

I am
afraid
this one
is not
so clear
as the

25

others. Just one more picture and then I must stop, I will send you a Microbe letter Tomorrow. I am

Sorry you did not get this one

Weel, La, La —

From Lettie

10 Chamonry
Old Aberdeen

12ᵗʰ Feb 1903

My dear Miss Dorothy!

I am sorry this microbe letter was not written yesterday as I promised, but better late than never. I am now going to draw you a Tumyache microbe. The Tumyache is not quite the same as other microbes, he does not catch people, they catch him. I think I have heard you say, "Oh! dear I have got a Tumyache! and I do'nt believe you."

27

liked him one bit.

He feeds on jam and sweets
and cake, and all that sort
of thing ; and the stuff he
hates most of all is Castor-oil.
Now, as I have still a big
~~space~~ piece of paper left
I will tell you about the
Small-pox microbe. he is very

small - (you see that by his name,) but very dangerous.

It is best to keep always well out of his way, he is so small, he can go where bigger microbes would not be able to.

now I must stop.
I hope you will like this letter — Love from
                                  Lettie.

By 1909, Letty was a rebellious, self-willed young woman of twenty-nine, who, sandwiched between four brothers, had no romantic illusions about the male sex, which she incidentally vastly preferred. Her young sister, Dorothy, was sixteen at this time and was always referred to as 'the kid', a hangover from an upbringing partly in America.

It was suggested at the Convent in Aberdeen that she pursue her interest in art and manuscript illumination, at which she was very talented, and moved to teach drawing at a Sacred Heart Convent in Wandsworth. Her work bears witness to that talent.

Illuminated Manuscript by Lettie

St Petersburg

Lettie at last realised herself that she had a vocation but mentioning it to her family raised an instant storm. One elderly relative told her that the matter with her was that she had not enough to do! Faced with this accusation, Letty wrote to an old governess, who was then in Russia, asking if she could find her a post teaching English there. This the governess managed to do, and in March 1909, Letty set off as Governess to the Paltoff family who lived at Tsarskoe-Selo near St. Petersburg, in the Circle of Czar Nicholas II.

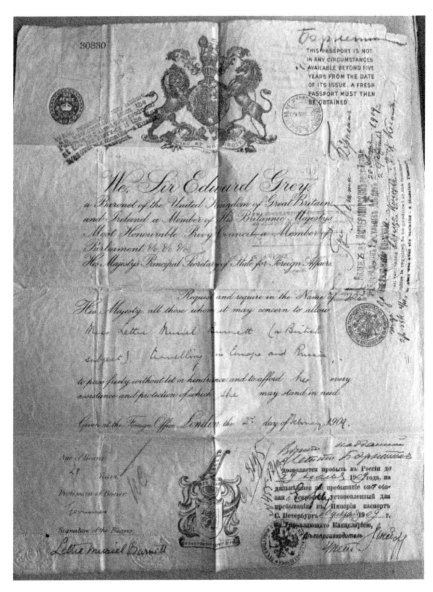

Lettie's Visa for Russia

The post cards and letters she wrote home during her time there are interesting. She was twenty-nine and it was an adventure for somebody of her age. The Catherine Palace at Tsarskoe Selo was the summer residence of the Imperial family and visiting nobility. It had its name changed to Detskoe Selo, translated maybe appropriately as the Children's Village, in 1918 following the revolution, and then again to Pushkin in 1937. The postcard below is of Peterhof, June 20th the Summer Palace of Peter the Great.

Miss D Burnett
Cheltenham College
Angleterre

Feb 27 Thursday

Dear D

I shall write to you next week and tell you about this new place I've gone to. It is half hour by train from St Petersburg where the Tsar now lives.

A boy and girl 12 and 13. The boy has a tutor.

This PC is one of the smaller chateaux near St Petersburg. Not very beautiful, but I like the fountains. Rather interested to hear of <u>your</u> news! "Your" in this case being used in the plural. Tell Gwen! Compris?

Best love

LMB

However much kindness Lettie delivered, she was frank and prepared to speak her mind. Maybe we should describe it as honesty!

We don't know the identity of Gwen or some of the persons named in the next letters.

C/o Madame Paltoff
Serednaia Oulitza No 12
Tsarskoe Selo
Nr St Petersburg

March 2 – 15

Dearest Mum

I arrived here yesterday. Miss Wilson very kindly escorted me a short half hour from St P the little town about as large as Stonehaven very good air and no cholera, (I am sure that is wrongly spelt!). This is a large house and I have a nice room always without carpets, which is such an uncomfortable idea don't you think?

But it is their way in these parts evidently. Madam is rather a fashionable lady! About 40, not more. The two children seem nice. The boy is nearly 13, very ugly but a nice face and his sister 11 and rather pretty and a bit of a monkey I gather. Her mother told me she wished her to get out of her tomboy manners!

Pa I haven't seen yet. There is a German youth, the boy's German tutor, who takes charge of him all morning till after lunch, then goes out for classes himself and returns at 6:30 for dinner.

They seem to do themselves pretty well in the way of servants and they have a man to wait, in fact I should put the house down as a sort of sometime Aunt .. ..establishment !! Breakfast at 8:20- which is coffee. At 8:30 the little girl goes off to School. 12.30 lunch. I am free all morning except for an hour's lesson to Madame! After lunch 2 till 4 a walk, sometimes with both children, at other times with the girl alone. At 4 Tea, 4.30 – 5.30 English lesson for the two of them. 5.30 - 6.30 they have preparation. Dinner is at 6.30. I am told no one dresses for dinner in Russia except for a dinner party! From 7.15 to 8.30 Games and at 8:30 there is tea again for the children. 9.00 Bed and I am free again from about 9.30 or 10. Twice a week I am to give them a drawing lesson. I have never seen a child draw so well as the little boy here, his things are really wonderful. My pay is £6 per month. Unfortunately I do not know German so I can't converse with the German youth as he does not speak a word of French or English; Very few Russians it seems speak English, it has just become the fashion.

What a bother Miss Louisa is. I hope she isn't going to fall through like this at the last moment, what difference can it make who she takes the house from? I do hope Vernon Pirie has been able to do something for Doodie, I am afraid he will leave unless he gets something at once, it seems awful folly to me. I must really write to Hilda, I am glad she is staying on with the Georges. I was awfully afraid she would be running back to London. I suppose she gave me that idea as Doodie had to go to Cork.

Remember to tell me how Robin is when you write again. I hope he is not down with fever. Miss Faithful's letters were extremely nice. It was very good of her to get the kid into the Foundation. Isn't she in a high state of delight?

By the way the name of the people here is Paltoff. I have given you the right address this time but if you have written, the other will find me alright. All Russian names and addresses have to be translated into English as near as possible by the sound as many of the letters are different.

Hope Tom will be able to sell his motor cars! I haven't seen many about here yet, the snow is still rather much for them; no more news at present. It has got rather colder again but it can't last much longer now we are into March

Best love your ever affectionate daughter,

Lettie M Burnett

Whilst Lettie fulfilled her role as the children's governess, she by no means forgot what was happening back at Kemnay which was going through a difficult financial period. She was clearly concerned about what is happening to the family home, and no doubt fully aware of the problems created by her grandfather, and later by her father.

It does appear that Miss Wilson was her old governess who introduced her to St Petersburg and that she stayed with the Gelbe family when she first arrived there.

Lettie seldom forgot her dog Bacchus

C/o Madame Paltoff
Serednaia Oulitza No 12
Tsarskoe Selo
Nr St Petersburg

Monday

My dearest Mum

Many thanks for yours.

First. The Papers for Milligan arrived. I signed these and registered and sent them back the day after, on Wed the 17th, so he should have got them yesterday or today.

Well! You can breathe in peace at last having got more out of these then I ever thought you would, but what a time of waiting and worry when it all could've been done months ago. "Barra and the £600" is too delightful, you should be quite comfortable on that and your own!! I wonder who started it. It will have probably grown to £800 by this time question!!

A letter from Doodie yesterday telling me he was going to stick on till the end of April as he had not given up all hope yet of getting something. Have you heard from Robin since you wrote? You are rather afraid he was down with fever again as he hadn't written for some time.

You will have got my letter written today after I arrived here, just a week ago telling you what sort of house and people I had fallen among this time! It was Miss Wilson who heard of these people and told them of me, she has really been very kind; she and her brother wanted me to leave the Gelbes and go into the Governess Home the first week I was here, but that would have been extremely stupid and I would have lost £10 straight off and my board at the Home as well.

39

As it was, I only had £5 to pay the Gelbes back. £4-10/- I had and these the Paltoffs advanced me 30 /- I did my first month for journey expenses out here (which were only about 6/-!) and so I managed most satisfactorily don't you think!

Madam Paltoff improves our acquaintance, also that she does not always wear ……..!!! But the child is a handful! The mother, I am glad to say she knows it which makes matters more easy. She is only 11, but clever for her age and very sharp; her name is pronounced "Xseneur". How it is spelt is quite another matter and beyond me! I have not much to do with the boy which I'm quite glad he does not seem to be any more angelic than his sister. However, I have got over the first week without any tears on Xseneur's part which I believe is good so far. I must say I should like to have smacked her once or twice! especially when just by way of a little "fuss", she left two teeth marks on my arm!!! However, she may improve. I've only been here nine days and she can be a nice kid when she wants to.

Yesterday we went into St Petersburg and lunch with the Grand-Ma and then went to a museum of pictures.

I am at a great disadvantage not speaking German as both tutor and housekeeper speak only Russian and German and of course I cannot trust the children to translate for me! I think I must try and pick up a little German – I'll tell you next week how I have got on with the two little devils!

And now for your bit of family news - I was glad to hear my cousins were off at last. Poor Uncle Arthur ! ! but if he is nice well learned! and rich, she hasn't done badly for herself. When is it to be? I wrote my congrats off at once; mercy on us!! Think of Puff and Ida likened to the aunts it must really be a case of blind affection on their father's part.

A letter from Mrs Hayes partly unreadable! Saying you were looking – is it "white" or "well"? I hope not the first. If so recuperate!

Now the beastly business of deeds and documents is over, you can sleep in peace as far as they are concerned. Are Doodie and Tom now ready for the revenge on Reed?!

I must send this up now. Tell Amy the fur boots <u>have</u> been and are most valuable, (the ones she gave me). You seem to have the most awful weather. Of course, here is still a white world but the frost is beginning to go.

I got the free press today and have just seen the death of F Angus. I saw him when I stopped at Amy's. It seems to have been quite sudden from what the paper says. Poor old man. He had been ill for long time.

Don't send on any more of these RC papers I will try to stop there.

Kiss Bachie from me and tell him I hope he and Becky are friends! was very glad to hear he had got over his sick turn

Best love from your affectionate daughter Lettie M Burnett .

P.S. I hear there is "another little" Crosswit and "is doing very well"! (Not really ....sometime now) .

P.S. I knew Mrs Paton would have a fit!!!

Understandably, Easter has an extra special place in Lettie's heart.

Easter Monday.

My dearest Mum

The great Day is over! It began on Saturday night at 11.30 when the whole Russian world goes off to Church. I had an invitation to go with Madame Paltoff who went to the Palace Church, evening dress white and high for the woman, full dress uniform for the men. The Palace is gold and blue, a magnificent place - every two steps a lackey in scarlet and gold - we were shown from one ante room into another, all in dead silence - till we got to the Church - I should never have known it was a Church, just a room on first sight - very high and lit entirely by candles – most wonderful colour, panels of sapphire blue and raised gold, not at all gaudy or 'tinsellie' as is generally the effect of much gold. But wonderfully beautiful, a frescoed ceiling - and at the far end three golden doors, one great large one in the centre; Behind these doors is the altar and in the Greek Church, half the service is carried on behind these shut doors, at parts the doors are opened, and one can see then what is going on. The priests have long hair, parted in the middle and falling to their shoulders, also long beards.

At a few minutes to midnight, the golden doors opened and out came a procession of six footmen carrying an Icon, a cross, two banners and two lanterns, followed by the priests, the choir and joined by a large number of the congregation all holding lighted candles. We were all given these candles on coming into Church. This procession made a tour of the Palace "In search of Christ" and returned singing

42

"Christ is risen".'

The priest then turned to the people and said three times "Christos Voskrest" which is Christ is risen and everyone replied three times with the same words. Then the candles are put out and they all started falling in on each other's necks and embracing three times on each cheek. I got off with two such salutations but some of the people must have gone into three numbers! After this was all over, they went on with the service. We went away at a 1:45 and it wasn't finished then. It was very tiring standing the whole time. There were no seats at all.

The Emperor was not there. We were in the big palace which is used for all functions of state receptions etc. He lives in the small palace about a five minute walk from the large one and receives no one there. I was sorry as I should have liked to have seen him near at hand.

There was not a single man last night not in uniform and most of them covered with medals, orders, stars, ribbons etc. They pile them on in Russia! When we returned to the house at 2.a.m. we sat down to a large dinner with many guests. We began with hard-boiled eggs and ended up with a sour milk cake! They have any number of queer eatables some of it you would like. Beetroot soup with whipped cream for one is an odd dish.

I had a note from Nora the other day, she is off to Oxford at last. Do hope you are better than when you were with Amy. You must have had a horrid bad turn. I quite understand the difficulties of enjoying a visit to Amy now. You don't know where you are with Fotheringham on such a strange footing. Poor you, you must have been bad to have been asked to play at cards! I cannot imagine you playing. How you must have loathed it!

43

Love to Tom and the kids. Any good news of Doodie yet? The kid here is better and went downstairs yesterday. The tutor is away for a week, so I have both children on my hands just now.

Must end. Much love

Your ever affectionate Lettie M Burnett

PS Could you send these papers to "Convent" (The Mother Superior)

Note: Nora is the daughter of Surgeon Major James Macdonald from Aberdeen and sister of Sir James Ronald Leslie Macdonald, explorer, cartographer and British Army Engineer.

Nora was a skilled photographer, illustrator and curator with an expertise in ancient and modern languages. She became fascinated with Egypt and archaeology and eventually married the renowned Egyptologist, Francis Griffith at Oxford during the year of this letter. When she died, she left her two terriers and her Welsh dresser to Lettie's sister, Dorothy.

Postcard Troika

Serednaia Oulitza No 12

Tsarskoe Selo

Nr St Petersburg

To Miss D Burnett

C/o Mrs Euan

Deepsmay

Tiverton

Devon

Tuesday April 29th

Salutations to ....and yourself

How would you like to have one of these for your private carriage?

LMB

Whilst many of the names mentioned in the letters mean little or are illegible, Lettie maintained her interest in what was going on at home.

C/o Madame Paltoff
Serednaia Oulitza No 12
Tsarskoe-Selo
Nr St Petersburg

No date

My dearest Mum

Your letter received two days ago after being kept about a week at Tsarskoe before forwarding on here. I was very glad to have news again as it was a whole long month since I heard from you.

We have been here in Inverskaia Goubernica about a fortnight and return to Tsarskoe tomorrow, then leave for Germany (I don't know what town but not Baden-Baden) on the 21st I believe. I will send you my address from there, but if you write before, write to the Tsarskoe address.

Was I ever so taken aback in my life as at Nora's news! -Never!! I heard from Miss ..... before that he was "delightful and of course fearfully learned. I asked her if she had broken the news to Uncle Jack!! Glad you think Ida's little man is nice. Don't go and give away any of your nice old things to them "in a present ."

I hope Uncle A.... and Aunt P.... will have enough sense to let Nelly go back to Germany. They will have fine house if Puff and she are at home together and if the child has such a good voice and really wants to go back, why on earth do they wish to prevent her. Things seem to be going well with that part of the family anyway!

Addie passed her exams and with work after her own heart, Ida married to a nice young man and Nelly keen on music, just tell the old man he needn't grumble!

About Doodie I feel just as Sybil said "I can't talk about it. " I am sorrier than I can say, can't get it out of my head - I had imagined him, all sorts of honour and glory and silly things in the future. I wonder what he thinks of doing – may he do anything rather than marry Hilda. Mummy always used to say that would never be. I trust she was right.

What can I tell you of this place - about 12 Verst from the small station halfway to Moscow. Miles and miles and hundreds of miles of uncultivated ground, rich in forests of pine and birch, miles of waving grass and wildflowers every kind, no roads to call roads, only "farm tracks"! Houses big and small of wood. I asked if there were any old Palaces in this part of the country and was told of one house belonging to a proprietor that was 50 something years!! They never build in stone. Most of the houses about were burnt down by the peasants three years ago when the country was in such a state!

The peasants are nearly always drunk whenever they have a few pence. Do you know it is not 50 years since they were slaves, it seems extraordinary. The feeling of this huge wild land is strange, so unlike anything I have ever seen before. We have a small wooden house quite near to Mrs P's brother "Colonel Kalsackoff" (I spell as pronounced!) We only sleep in our house and come back here to feed. Oh straw beds are very uncomfortable! But mosquitoes are worse. The first night we have arrived I showed my ignorance to the full by leaving our window open, it was so awfully hot. Result - I was attacked by hundreds of thousands of mosquitoes as I had only a thin sheet, the devils eat me all over, I got up and walked up and down, thought I

47

should get mad. In the morning I hardly knew myself!!! Now the windows are tight shut and I suffocate in peace.

I'm glad we're going to Germany but only for three or four weeks then back to St P for a marriage then again on the way to Cannes I think.

Sorry you have been so long without a letter, but I waited to get yours - Gosh I can't imagine Nora engaged!

My love to Evelyn when you see her next. France would never never have done!

How is Bacchus? Must end and go and see what the child is up to. Mrs P told me the other day it was the fault of all her governesses but they didn't "s' àttache à Xenia". Amusing if you knew the child. I felt inclined to say what do you know about your kids, you only see them five minutes a day! I have a fellow feeling for their former governesses I didn't "àttache" !! For the present things are going pretty smoothly. She has given up biting anyway you can tell Mrs Paton!

Best love. Your ever affectionate daughter. Lettie Burnett

C/o Madame Paltoff
Serednaia Oulitza No 12
Tsarskoe-Selo
Nr St Petersburg

April 25-May 8th

Dearest Mum

Never very much news to give you. I got two of these "d…..d paperies" from Milligan to sign, which I did and sent them back the same day, Friday 7th, to be sent onto the other "Misses Burnetts" to sign. You might mention to him from me next time you see him that his clerk might make a note of the fact I have changed my address! from Crestovsky Selo to Tsarskoe Selo! It would save the chance of things getting lost if has any more papers to send. I gave them my new address when ……papers over …weeks ago and am childishly delighted I can jump on a lawyer body like Milligan for risking the safety of our precious documents! Letters have a way of straying in this country at times., if you give them the chance.

Xenia goes back to school on Monday. I'm thankful to say she says she loves me now. The depth of her affection is wonderful. She took another bite of my arm the other day and is rather proud of the fact! The boy at times forgets he hates me. He is so ugly I really rather like him, a nice gentle lad! He told me this evening that his father had promised him a bulldog and he was going to teach it to fly at me! He was so pleased I could not resist the temptation of telling him dogs were very friendly to me as a rule and I will keep a special store of sugar in my pockets to steal its affections from him.

Yesterday we went to a review of 10,000 troops.

They were nearly all young soldiers of the line and not very interesting except because of the great number. There are only about 800 cavalry.

Last night we went with the children to some private theatricals and Xenia sat next to the Grand Duchess Olga (sister of the Emperor) who chatted to her. I had a good look at her; she is young, about 30 pale and badly dressed, but has a very nice face.

We also saw a review of sailors last week. They were very smart. The Emperor whom I saw quite close that day walk down the line of about two or three hundred officers and spoke to each one.

I watched him at least half the time and not once did he smile, very white faced and worn looking, with a funny quick way of looking round without moving his head. Not so like the Prince of Wales as I had thought. The Empress I should think had been very beautiful, but she has the saddest face I've ever seen. They do not like her in Russia even amongst the aristocracy. They say she is cold.

Last night last Sunday I went to St Petersburg and made for the inside of St Isaac. The pillars I shouldn't like to risk a guess of how high, are of lapis lazuli and beautiful green stone malachite and are perfectly beautiful. I could have stayed and looked at them for ages. They get the stone, malachite, and many others from Siberia.

I believe we start for Germany in the last week in June and, when Madame P has finished drinking the nasty waters there, go on to Florence which will be really delightful.

Your loving and affectionate daughter,

Lettie Burnett

50

Fri June 3rd

My dearest Mum

Your letter this minute received. Many thanks for it and last week's which I have not, I'm sorry, answered before. These last days we seem to have been very much on the trot; Now the schools are closed, I have my time pretty much taken up with herding Xenia!

I sent you a PC from a place we spent the day at on the borders of Finland. It was really very pretty there and lots of firs made the place look more summerie. The trees this last week have come out with a rush and some of them are looking quite green which is a comforting sight!

We leave this next week and go to Madame P's brothers for a fortnight I think and hope, if I am in luck, to see Moscow. All letters will be forwarded, I will send you new addresses when I know these myself. Many thanks for the book on Florence, it will be of great use. I shall read it up beforehand and mark what I most want to see.

I was glad to hear you had got the move over at last and how thankful you must be. What a perfectly awful packing you must've had. Miss Louisa, I hope, is properly thankful to you for getting papering etc. done for her and the house already to step into, I should think she would take an easy first class for worrying! She surely can't have been like that when she was head of Saint Leonards!

I got an amusing letter from Mrs Paton saying she thought Mr Leslie's dog would be anything but blessed by Louisa!

51

She is a fidget. However if she keeps the place "as - she -would - be - done - by-", it should be super perfect.

I was awfully taken aback the other day by a present from Madame Paltoff of a dressing case! fitted up and just large enough to hold things for a night; an awfully nice one and just the thing for travelling. It was most awfully kind of her, but I was surprised.

I don't see very much of her she's always out, but what I do see I like.

Well, what a mercy the Kemnay matters are at last settled and how sickening having to spend the remainder of your £250 on law expenses; I should just think you were glad to have finished with it all and well you have done to get as much as you have out of them, but I should love to be able to visit Reid and leave him bodily incapable. Here I fully sympathise with Tom and Doodie.

Is there any good news for Doodie yet? And is Tom still down! South? I am so glad about Paul, poor old thing. If the secret sale! Didn't pay up things enough for her, let me send you £5. It would keep her another week in the home and I would like to help and I have got the money or will have on the 14th.. The longer she stays in the home the stronger she will be to go back to the old sisters.

My £14-2-0 can just stay with D.G. Don't you think of making it up.

Please pay up my small bills out of the £3 only if any small ones you don't know about come in. You had better wait till you get at my receipt in August. Tell me if you do want my boxes of anything else paid up later. It's no use to your being out of pocket for my bills.

I was glad to hear of the death of that poor child, the best thing that could've happened.

What are your plans? I see you are at Straloch. Mrs Paton said she was expecting you the 15th. Where are you going after that? And when will Gertrude be home!

Must end. Best love and a pet to Bacchus

Your ever affectionate Lettie M Burnett

C/o Madame Paltoff
Seredenia Oulitza No 12
Tsarskoe-Selo
Nr St Petersburg

Monday

My dearest mum

Many thanks for your letter and enclosed. Glad that Bacchus is better and again enjoying life. An Easter card arrived from Amy. I hope she was well enough to enjoy her birthday. You say nothing about yourself. Nana says you are looking rather done up when she saw you. She is now well started at Oxford. I expect grinding for all she is worth.

Not much news to give you from these parts. Snow again which is hateful and therefore colder. We saw a review of Lifeguards on Saturday and today a review of Cossacks. I did not think much of the first regiment and thought their cheers for the Emperor were lacking in fervour! But the Cossacks were very fine-three different

regiments "The Red" "The Blue." "The Yellow". entirely got up – uniforms, lances and saddles - in one of those colours-they make a very brilliant sight (I think I'd like the blue best). They were mounted on rather small horses with long manes and tails and go like the wind. These reviews take place in the huge square before the palace and the public are not allowed in; it was at one of these two years ago a soldier threw a bomb at the Emperor.

The whole of the royal family was there on Saturday. Today the Emperor and Empress and the little prince, he is only 4 1/2 but he looks older and at the reviews stands by himself and salutes the different regiments as they pass, in the most grown-up way!

Xenia is better and goes back to school tomorrow I am glad to say summer holidays begin the last day of May -t he middle of June at home – and last for 3 1/2 months! An awful long time isn't it? Madame Paltoff really is very nice. Of course, I don't see much of her and of General Paltoff hardly ever a sight. He seldom comes home till the small hours. He has some very good state appointment but what it is I can't quite find out!! Something to do with engineering, I think. What I have seen of him I don't care much about. He is very ugly, looks bad tempered and I should think is conceited. If I get a chance of photos of any of them, I shall send you them home to see what the family is like!

I am going into St Petersburg next Sunday to the Hermitage. I believe the pictures they're very fine. I did not care at all for the collections at the other museums I have seen.

Any news of Doodie? Does Tom know his plans further? What will he do if he goes east again? He can't rejoin the Bombay B Co. can he?

What a bit of luck, the Gardens buying Uncle Charles's house. Do you know what price it is going out? That is a really good bit of news. I thought tenements would be the sure fate of that field. The fir wood at Barra I am glad has been thrown in. The private grounds are not very large! Remember to send me a schedule of the plans what an awful time you will have moving; number 10 is not exactly a large house, but there is a very good amount of stuff in it!

I have such a beast of a pen. It refuses to do anything but make blots. The kid seems to be getting on A1 at school how she does love it. I wonder what steps Miss Faithful is taking about St Austin's. Do you think they will find Mrs Ridley gone when they return from the holidays? You will find it a difficult job to get a good gardener for Evelyn, when does she come to Caskieben. I too am thankful Hilda is staying abroad. I heard from Doodie she was going to Germany. I wish she would find a nice man there!

Goodbye Love to Tom and yourself. I must write to Mrs Paton.

Many thanks for the tips about the food. They have all sorts of queer things!

Ever your affectionate daughter

Lettie M Burnett

Lettie complained of the quality of her pen. Whether she was being economical or there was a shortage of writing paper, most of her letters contain little wasted space and most have the final lines written along the edge at right angles to the earlier lines and on occasions written on top of them!

C/o Madame Paltoff
Serednaia Oulitza No 12
Tsarskoe-Selo
Nr St Petersburg

Monday May 4th 11th

My dearest Mum

How goes the world with you at No 10. It is over a fortnight since I heard from you, but I hope you are in the throes of packing. Is Bacchus a very miserable little dog? Oh!

I saw in the paper that Principal Laing was dead and that they had to make out the poor old man had been a popular Principal. I am sorry for Mrs Laing poor thing. I wonder if she will go and live with the Semple Lad - he is wifeless.

A letter from Doodie - nothing for him yet – and one from Sybil praying the "Gods' may hear her and send a fair young German to Hilda" if she only could find one. Doodie sent me her address and I must try and write for her birthday, only I forget it is the 22nd of May or June?!

Madam Paltoff has been away for a few days but comes back this evening. She went off to Berne to see a friend who was very ill and helped the daughter, who is quite young girl, nurse him. However, he died under the operation before she arrived - cancer. I saw the man only a fortnight ago at dinner here and he looked quite alright, but I was told he had been ill for a long time.

General Paltoff was also at Berne, but fortunately the children have done nothing especially wicked while their mother has been away!

No excitement of any sort this week, not even reviews to tell you about! I have not got on very far with Russian - but can I ask for what I want, but don't understand a word when a conversation is going on. You see one has not much chance to pick it up so much French is spoken - every Russian of the better class knows French and most of them, as well as their own language and German runs it very close. English comes in a bad third, but it is becoming fashionable as the Emperor's children are learning to speak it! I can find my way about and buy a ticket and do a little shopping! but in a very elementary fashion.

Enclosed is a postal order for £3.3/- to pay Watt and Milne, Cruickshanks and Pratt and Keith. I think it should be about right as far as I can remember. Would have sent it before, if I had not to refund my journey to the Gelbkes !

Must end with best love to go out walking with the child!

Ever your affectionate daughter

Lettie M Burnett

Postcards

Miss D Burnett

St Austins

Cheltenham College

Cheltenham

June 1st 09

Его Императорское Высочество Насл̀дникъ Цесаревичъ,
и Великiй Князь,
АЛЕКСѢЙ НИКОЛАЕВИЧЪ.

The Little Prince (Tsarevich Alexei Nikolaevich)

This is very good of him. He is only 4 years old and looks about 6.

When do your holidays begin? Thanks so much for your many letters? I think I wrote last - By the way, many congrats on your place in the Const & Ex

Salutations to Gwen and yourself.

58

I am still in Tsarskoe but expect to be going to the country next week. I have been in Finland since I last wrote. It is much prettier than this part of Russia which is awfully flat. Hope to see Moscow with luck. We are going in that direction and 12 hours by train in this country is counted as nothing.

Adieu L.M.B.

C/o Madame Paltoff

Serednaia Oulitza No 12

Tsarskoe-Selo

Nr St Petersburg

Sunday, June 20 1909

My dearest Mum

Many thanks for your last letter. You will be at Mrs Paton's now and hope you will be able to outstay Aunt Pen and send her back to the Den without you! I don't expect Mrs Paton will let you go once you are there. As you see by my address, we are still at Tsarskoe only I believe we are really going off this week. Only when and where first I do not know. If we go to the country it will only be for a fortnight at most and then somewhere in Germany.

I wrote to Nana about three weeks ago. Am very sorry she has no more babies in prospect. What is Helen about! It is a serious matter for Nana if her legs are giving way, I hope the rest will put that right.

Are there not any new people to have babies? Have the "Crosswits" come to an end at last? I don't think Nana has ever been without a babe on the horizon before.

What sort of job has Tom got? Motor line? Or anything he likes? I had a letter from Nora the other day. She seems up to her ears in work, but if she goes North, I hope she will be able to take herself away from her books! to see Barra. It sounds delightful, and how nice of Mrs Irvine doing up the little top room.

This past week I have been a sight! I tried to break my nose playing tennis and have been a beautiful sight ever since, with a cut across the bridge which makes me like Uncle Charles! And two eyes of deep purple!!

By the way. how did you like the photos I sent you? I thought it was rather a good one. It would be very nice if Sybil took up her abode at Inverugie. No way for her to motor over, if the motor didn't break down!

No news this week. Hope to know soon for certain when we leave this and where we are going.

Yes. I believe Mrs P does like me which is a good thing.

Best love always your affectionate daughter

Lettie M Burnett

'The Tsar's village' was a world apart, an enchanted fairyland to which only a small number of people had the right of entry. Outside the palace gates, Tsarskoe Selo was an elegant provincial town dominated by the life and gossip of the court. The mansions of the aristocracy, that lined the wide tree-shaded boulevard which led from the railway station to the gates of the Imperial Park, pulsed with the rhythm emanating from the Imperial household.

The Tsar and his family led a simple, rigidly regulated domestic life in one wing of the Alexander Palace, a little house built by Alexander 1 following the defeat of Napoleon, but which nevertheless contained over a hundred rooms. Tatiana, the second daughter of the Tsar, was twelve in 1909 and Marie, who was ten, had an English governess, Miss Eager. There is no mention in her letters of a private tea party at the Imperial Palace, but Lettie would have felt very much at home in the Anglicised schoolroom. She did receive a crested cup and saucer which was always given as a memento to those who had been included in the domestic life of the Imperial family.

Crested Cup and Saucer

The extracts from Lettie's letters should be placed against the background of their period. We can see the day to day life of a young woman living at the epicentre of history, yet not taking any special interest in the undercurrents pulling her world into the maelstrom of revolution. Yet discernible they are in her day to day comments.

Bad Homburg von die Höhe was known for its medically used mineral water and spa and also for its casino, neither of which would appeal to Lettie.

Hotel Bellevue
Bad Homburg
Germany

August 3rd

Dearest Mum

We stay here till Monday then go elsewhere, place unknown as yet. Perhaps St Jean de Lutz.

I saw the "Zeppelin" come down to Frankfurt two days ago - Wonderful thing it is.

Will write on Thursday when M Paltoff joins us here as I shall then be able to tell you where we are going.

This is a view of the town, a nasty fashionable place, but the old part of it is rather pretty. Uncertain weather. One day 100° in the shade, the next rain and cold.

One drink of the smellie water was enough for me! I've got a vile cold in the head.

Have you seen G F S yet and has N M arrived in these parts. Looking forward to a letter soon.

They are too awful about forwarding letters from Russia yet. I can give you no other certain address at present. In true Russian fashion they think does not matter now or a week hence when things are seen to.

We will return to Tsarskoe sooner than that had at first been arranged probably the end of September, but one never know. Plans may be changed again a hundred times. On the whole I think I prefer to be in Tsarskoe for the winter. My cold has addled my brain.

Adieu. Your loving affectionate daughter

Lettie Burnett

Houlgate is another fashionable tourist resort with a beach and casino. It was unlikely to be to Lettie's liking, but her letter does tell us that her commitment to Catholicism was her underlying priority.

~~Hotel du Casino~~
~~Houlgate~~
~~Calvados~~

C/o Madame Paltoff
Serednaia Oulitza No 12
Tsarskoe-Selo
Nr St Petersburg

Aug 30 09

My dearest Mum

Many thanks for your letter received yesterday. At this moment, I think of you as probably suffering in the hands of the dentist. I hope the last ones weren't awful to get out, but I am afraid you will only think of "sops" tonight and for some days to come.

We leave this on Wednesday (in two days) then via Paris and Berlin straight to Tsarskoe where we were all due on the 4th for a wedding (always weddings!). This one is Mrs P's nephew and an important function, as the Emperor is to be there on the part of the bride who is daughter of Gupkin Head of I M's household.

I'm very sorry not to have seen Italy, but for some things shall be glad of the return to Tsarskoe as I shall have more time and I think I shall take, or rather give, an extra lesson in the mornings, which should give me a few more Rbles! I could quite easily fill my time in St Petersburg or Tsarskoe giving lessons by the hour, which is very well-paid; and, if I had been staying on, should have done so, as it is much more pleasant having one's own room than living in a family I should think, but this would be death to the drawing and so to the Convent plan for a year.

To see how it goes with the illumination, the Rev Mother holds it open till I see her, to accept or refuse. Of course, it is only on the condition of my having time for any illumination that I take the post, the holidays are the ordinary English ones.

This - as you will see by the date, was begun on the 30th it is now the third and we are back at Tsarskoe. I have not had a moment till now in which to finish it. We made out the journey alright via Paris, Berlin two nights three days and I've packed for everyone except Monseiur! " Madame P had with her about 20 dresses, not counting blouses. Oh goodness! Never again! She packed her hats. It took her all afternoon!

Tsarskoe is looking its best. Blue sky and dry, but there is a cold nip in the air which says winter is not far off. Xenia begins her lessons on the 1st September that is the 13th with us and then I should be free in the mornings again to my great delight. She is about the same, a kid that doesn't care for anyone really. Michael at least, after much patience, I have made friends with. He is not an angel but a sight better than his sister! Xenia talks English pretty well now and understands or reads anything you like to give her, which I think is pretty good for 6 months especially as no one talks English in the House except me – but German, Russian or French always.

Goodness how these children are spoilt, Fancy giving a kid of 11 50 francs one day and then 20 marks another and so on- that child had about Fr.100 francs in six weeks which I saw her father and mother give her, the secret of half their cussedness is simply they are blasé at the age of 11 or 12 ! Toys, horses, dogs, bicycles motoring, travelling – theatres, restaurants, champagne, it is really wicked. The boy asks for a watch – gets it- the girl – a dressing case- she gets it. etc.

65

The mother would give them the moon if she could get it. She, poor dear, is about the weakest person I ever set eyes on – but mercy, how she can spend. We had a few hours in Paris and she went shopping – one hat 200 francs, one costume 360 francs etc., but enough of that.

I found when I arrived here, a letter waiting from the Mother Superior telling me she had left Wandsworth for Roehampton but saying that this need not make any difference to my taking the post at Wandsworh. I am sorry she will not be there. She did not tell me who had taken her place, but as Roehampton is also, I believe, a suburb, I can go and see her when I am in London and arrange things there.

I can't remember did I tell you, we had been in Mont St Michel before we left Normandie, wonderful place. I would have given much more for another night there, but of course I sent you PCs of the place, I am dottling. Good night. Much love dearest Mum.

Ever you aff: daughter

Lettie M Burnett

In Scotland, where Lettie was born and brought up, history hangs about the shoulders like a cloak. Those who live under the shadow of Bennachie are not quite sure whether it was Celts or the mountain itself which swallowed up the legendary IX Roman Legion. Territorial boundaries are still marked in stone for permanence. Castle folk and cottage folk alike, conscious of the climate, build their houses with good deep stone walls, their backs frequently windowless and shrugged against the North wind.

In Russia Lettie seeks such solid antiquity in vain. "The spirit of serfdom still hangs about a bit. In the days of serfdom, the serfs were referred to as 'souls' and you reckoned the value of an estate by the number of 'souls' on it. Dead souls are dead serfs."

Imperial Russia, in the final phase of peace, constituted a large-scale experiment in state collective capitalism, and apparently a highly successful too. This alarmed the Germans, and the rapid growth of Russia was the single biggest factor in deciding Germany for war in 1941. When Lenin inherited the State Capitalist machine in 1917, it was to German wartime economic controls he looked for guidance.

The Russian tradition of peasant collectivism based on the commune and the craftsman's co-operative was sanctioned by the Orthodox church. Private enrichment was against the communal interest, though Socialisation and Nationalisation were words for which the peasants had no vocabulary. They just wanted a bit of land. This was natural enough. Steps taken since 1861 to create peasant proprietors whetted their appetites, however, led to rural agitation in 1905 and a revolution which was nipped in the bud. The acceleration of de-collectivisation was pursued faster after 1905 in order to boost food supplies to the towns, thus accelerating the industrialisation of Russia. In the decade before the First World War, Russian agricultural production was rising, and the peasants were getting better educated and began investing in industrial technology.

Lettie refers to her Aunt Frances. Totally ruled by her elder sister, Amy, Frances must have had a sad life. Whenever Amy considered that Frances had been naughty, she was shut up in a top room at Kemnay which was said to be haunted as a result of a past suicide.

This terrified poor Frances. Amy would not even allow her to attend any school and taught her what she thought was necessary. Sadly, Frances had a natural gift for art, but was not encouraged.

Aunt Lettie (Letitia) was Lettie's father's elder sister. There is the occasional mention of Robin and Doodie. What they were doing at this age may be of great interest, but sight should not be lost of the fact that they both went on to have exceptionally successful military careers.

C/o Madame Paltoff

Serednaia Oulitza No 12

Tsarskoe-Selo

Nr St Petersburg

Oct 6th - Nov 24th 1909

My dearest Mum

Many thanks for yours of the 31st.

So Francis did come to see you after all! It really does seem a splendid chance for her going out now with her aunt to Elskin if she really wishes to.

It will be very stupid of her if she doesn't and as I said before, she is not a child now and she can go if she wishes and no excuse of fearing the journey alone or anything of that sort. Besides, if she is looking seedy it would probably do her a lot of good.

Yes Aunt Lettie always speaks of sister Amelia as "Aunt Starke" now - it is fearful! So Dot is expecting! That's news, what excitement if it should be a son, though I should much rather Alastair's wife should present the family with an heir than Artie's. As you say, he is so fat and she is such a poor little thing!

I had a letter from Mrs Paton today – somehow I don't think she has got my last letter to her, written about the same time as yours all went missing. It probably went to the same place as they did wherever that may be

Doodie has had his time fully occupied if he has done all the things he intended to since he left you. By now he must be at Rotterdam waiting for his ship to sail.

Must go

7th

My Dearest Mum

Last night we went to the circus in Saint Petersburg. It isn't a very good one for the town but the horses were beautiful. We went to the stables at half-time and saw them! It seems strange, but everyone goes, and certainly they are worth seeing, most beautifully kept, and the horses all with their noses to the crowd, dear beasties. I fed them with carrots! We didn't get back home till past midnight, rather late for small kids I think!

How much is astricaine at home, or other how much would a small hat be? Round and this sort of thing. More than 30/-?

In winter everyone wears them either sealskin or astric an, is that the way to spell it?)

You have beaten me as far as snow goes, though the weather is bad enough. We had our first snow four days ago, a shower, but since then has taken to raining again, and it is now so dark and dismal and dirty --it's enough to make a cat sick! It is a quarter to four now, and in another 10 minutes I shall have to light up -The days are getting so short. Only the 25th of October with us, it does seem odd being 13 days behind the rest of Europe! The idea of holding Christmas on the 8th of January and New Year's Day on the 13th is strange. By the way, turkey is not an Xmas dish here, but we eat goose I believe.

I have not heard from Nora for a bit but suppose that she is off to Egypt by now. She told me when she last wrote that they have decided to live in Cairo. It sounds very tame. I thought that they would at least hire a tomb for themselves in the desert!

Not a vestige of news to give you.

Next Sunday I really must try and go to Petersburg and have a look at the Hermitage. I have seen the Alexandra Museum but not got to the Hermitage with its Murillos. Another thing I must see is the inside of the Winter Palace, if I can get a permit from Dedulin (General V N Dedulin commandant of the palace) and then I shall have something to tell you about for I am afraid that my letters have been most dreadfully dull,

What do you think of Korvinkrokouskaia for a name? It is a girl I give lessons to twice a week in the mornings. She is a nice girl.

Well ta ta. Give stinky a pat for me

With best love dear mum

I don't think that it would be unchristian for Lettie to have a poor opinion of Amy. There is clearly no love lost. As Francie's niece, there was little that Lettie could do to make her life more bearable. Note that Frances is two years younger than Lettie despite being her aunt.

C/o Madame Paltoff
Serednaia Oulitza No 12
Tsarskoe-Selo
Nr St Petersburg

November 1st 1909

My dearest Mum

Many thanks for your letter of the 24th of October

One from Doodie just this minute arrived, tells me he is really started and should be in London just now. What a blessing you are really settled at last. I'm sure it is awfully pretty, even the sight I had of it in its old state showed great possibilities. Aren't you rather late in the year to do anything more to the garden? Uncle Jack said he has sent you bulbs and <u>stuff </u>for it. I should think it needed a good deal a good lot of working at, as far as I can remember, it was simply a wilderness with currant bushes.

I have not seen in the Scotsman on Isabel's death. It will be dreadful for her sister. They lived always together didn't they? If only Miss Cavendish had deceased last year! Aunt Lettie could've gone and lived with her Aunt Agnes of whom she is very fond I believe.

Of all the piffling idiots – Frances takes the cake! Remember she is 26 or is it 27 now? And she hasn't the courage to blow her nose without sister Amelia's permission. Let her be as fond of her sister as she likes, but if she goes on much longer in the way she has done since Aunt Stark's marriage, she will get softening of the brain! Do you think she kisses "brother Stark", every morning! I expect it was just as Doodie said about her postcard.

Great and exciting news for Dorothy and Gwen, about St Austin's - I hope they will like St Helens, suppose they go there after the Xmas holidays. The kid seems to have been working very well this last year. I wonder where she will come out in her next exams.

A letter from Amy today from the, (as you say), awful Hydro. How she can go there! However, she tells me the last fortnight has been much better and is allowed the free run of her pen. She tells me Hopie has a son, so she is now a great aunt, and that great sorrow reigns because the babe has not red hair. Pray. They should comfort themselves by the thought that it is quite wasted on a boy! and look forward to the still greater pleasure of a red headed daughter! Amy also gives me the interesting detail that "Hopie has turned out a good cow and, by her own account, could run Mrs Burnett of Powis close."

So Gertrude has got a tin house. What on earth is it like- one roomed?! I shouldn't think it was much good starting to put it up, this time of the year; makes me shiver to think of her.

It is quite true the Czar is going to St Petersburg next month. Monseiur Paltoff says the danger is awful and he is not apt to exaggerate things. I do trust nothing will happen but people seem very much afraid.

We are looking out our furs, I would <u>like </u>to wear mine already?! But the real cold is not here yet, however we cannot expect more than another fortnight, I'm afraid before it is upon us and then I think that it must be like what you had in America. Madame Beltoft was quite astonished when I told her the sea did not freeze at Aberdeen! I hadn't the chance of seeing it last winter, but she tells me it always does at Petersburg. Of course the Neva does and they have tramways across it all winter.

Must end. No news this week, the infant here remains calmer!

Love to Tom and Bacchus

And much to yourself

Your ever affectionate daughter,

Lettie M Burnett

Nov 23rd

Dearest Mum

Many thanks for yours of last week.

So you too are in the midst of winter weather. It is awfully cold here and I have taken refuge in the old buffalo  coat, fur boots and a hat that covers all but the tip of my nose. They say the winter is going to be a very severe one, which is unfortunate for us as this is a very difficult house to keep properly heated. Xenia and I go out in the sledge every afternoon. Her pony goes very well. In fact he tried to bolt with us the other day! But oh, it is cold driving – I find my fur lined gloves are no good. Woollen ones are the only things or these best of all. The cold must be something like what you had in America.

Last Tuesday we all went up to St Petersburg- It was the birthday of the kid's grandmother and we did a little sightseeing. Went to the Fort and saw the tombs of the Czars, then to the 'Ermitage' which we had only time to tear around. It is a perfectly fascinating place and such treasures to be seen. I must return alone to see the pictures. We passed through the Egyptian collection which seemed to me a nice one, only I had not time to look at the things. The collection of weapons and armour is quite wonderful.

Some are literally encrusted with jewels and most exquisite workmanship. I remember one present to some defunct Czar the scabbard green with emeralds and the hilt with huge diamonds; and Murillos and da Vinci and Luini and Velazquez and a score of others. The pictures must have as much time as I can give to them. I knew there were treasures, but did not dream of so many. Gertrude would enjoy the Hermitage.

Thank you so much. I should like the doggie diary. Mrs Haynes' letter was amusing when I made it out, but that took some time. I am glad that Sir R Macdonald has got some job – hope it is better than it sounds. It would be sad for him if it leads to nothing more.

It was £3 I sent, and my receipts were in a long envelope in the small writing desk in the dining room.

I am sorry I have left my letter till late this week and if I do not end up and run out and post it now, it will miss Tuesday's post – next week I will tell you about my ride !! At the present moment I am so stiff and sore, I can hardly sit down!

Love to Gertrude and a kiss for Bachus

Ever your affect: daughter   L M Burnett

Life at Tsarskoe-Selo does have its share of excitements and dramas. When all is considered, Lettie had quite a rounded experience during her time in Russia.

In addition to the day to day life looking after the Paltoff children, the world of the Imperial family, visits to other parts of the country, Germany and France, together with experiences such as

Easter, the Circus and the Hermitage, gave her a grounding in life that many of her contemporaries would envy. Doubtless, there was more which she did not include in these letters to her mother.

C/o Madame Paltoff
Serednaia Oulitza No 12
Tsarskoe-Selo
Nr St Petersburg

Tuesday Dec 7

Dearest Mum

Many thanks for yours of the 29th

Now Mrs Irvine is back at Straloch, I expect you will be tree cutting for the view you want from your drawing room window. I hope Gertrude has found a site for her house. The Moor of Dinnet sounds a cold place to be playing about in this weather.

Last week I had a novel experience – driving a troika by night. A troika is a three horse sledge in which the horses go to canter all the time instead of a trot. In the real country it would be still more delightful. At night somehow things look still whiter and one seems to go faster in the darkness and dead silence except for the bells on the horses.

Troika

We had an unfortunate accident with Xenia's little sledges the other day. The pony which had not been out for four days behaved like a devil! Kicked up and came down with one leg the wrong side of the shaft. I was driving and before I could get at his head, he fell over and broke the shaft. However, mercifully he wasn't hurt himself. Kourt, Ivaitch and Michael did something of the same sort yesterday. A screw gave way and the sledge swung round on the horse who promptly bolted. However, no harm came to them except that the sledge was broken up!

A chapter of accidents. Last week the man who looks after the horses fell from the roof of the stable and knocked his head and hurt his arm badly--However it turned out better than we had at first feared and he came back from the hospital today. It is what Robin would call a 'putrid' hospital he was there a whole day before he saw a doctor or got anything to eat.

Do you think Gertrude would like a peasant's shirt? They are beautifully embroidered down the front, neck and cuff and sometimes the tails are worn like this: Or would embroidery alone be better?

I hope you found Mrs Haynes better. She has had a bad time of it this year with rheumatics, said  she missed you being away from the Chanonry very much.

Can you send me Miss Bowanan's address at Ozec? I must write to her, also Paul's which I have lost.
Hope this week has brought a letter from Doodie and Robin. I expect he will have re-joined his ship by now.

Wasn't Bacchus wild to get back again from Straloch. Poor darling he is looking very aged.

Best love

Return to Britain

There is little correspondence following her time in Russia.

When Lettie went to the Convent, she was permitted to take with her nothing by way of material possessions. There may be no record of what happened to what she did own other than a chair which her brother-in-law, Quentin, bought from her.

The time for entering the Society of the Sacred Heart came nearer and nearer and still she had not told her family of her plans. On her return to London, she went to see Mother Walpole, who was then at Roehampton, and was accepted for noviceship. Her entrance date was August 1910, but she became ill, and it was postponed until June 1911.

In her memoirs, Letty gives no hint of what passed between herself and her Mother when the latter was told of her intentions.

Perhaps she wished to forget what was said, but she does say that no noviceship could have been happier than that of 1911 to 1913. 'How privileged I was to have for Novice Mistress, Mother D'Arcy. Without her great kindness and understanding I cannot imagine how I could have survived the noviceship. Never for a moment did I change my mind, but looking back, I see with painful clearness, how ignorant I was of even the elements of religious life and how wonderful was the patience of that dearest Mother.'

Roehampton

On September 28th 1913, Lettie received the habit and on the following day, she made her vows. Until 1918 she taught drawing at Roehampton, and then went for a year to Mount Anville in Dublin where her old friend Mother Walpole was Superior.

One who was a child there during that year writes; "During that year I grew to love Scotland from what I heard of it from Mother Burnett. She had physical and mental energy beyond the ordinary, including her walk, her manner of speech, her high ideals. I remember her chiefly for the encouragement she gave me….. she worked on the principle that if we had done the appointed work for the day, then we could hear interesting reading. In this way we covered much during the year. This encouraging method allowed us ten to twenty minutes for enthralling reading and from this year I date my interest in good reading and history…."

Her illustrated letters to her sister, Dorothy, continue, although the content was a little more adult. The names are not important. Midmar is in rural Aberdeenshire.

Friday

We finish our Retreat tomorrow! I have just got yours - so glad to hear from you. Please give my congrats to Hugh. I hope his father is properly proud of him! I dreamed that Community had all gone up (me too) to Midmar instead of here TW) for the Summer change and awful to confess - when I got there I could not remember where the rooms were!! except "This is the dining room convenient as it is just above the kitchen!! "though I don't think I was ever in the kitchen - in those days it would not have been allowed by Annie Gordon! Wouldn't she be astonished now to hear she would probably get no dinner if she did not go and make it herself!

This is really just to thank you darling for yours. How I wish you could see this place. BEAUTIFUL grounds right out in the country.

Near nobody except the farmers..... Nice big house has been added to both sides and top so it's large enough for us all. Must be a delight for the children.

Thank you for Beena's Address. Have just sent off one of your PPCs. Thank you too for all your answers. Forgive me it is old age as well as no brains.

In September 1919 Lettie went to Probation and Profession at the Mother House, the Villa Lante in Rome.

Her brother-in-law, Quentin Irvine, does write to his mother from Rome in 1920 shortly before Lettie's arrival back at the Convent.

My Darling Mother

Since I wrote, we have been to Lettie's ceremony, which was very interesting. But very alarming for me, as I was the only male and so was put in a chair by myself at the side of the altar, right under the cardinal's nose.

The service began at 8 a.m. and finished at 10 when a very hungry Deb and I were presented to Cardinal Merry Del Val, who had the gift of making you feel quite alright once you got started; his mother was English and he was educated near Durham.

Lettie looks very thin but seems cheery; she must have been awfully bad and at the mercy of Italian doctors; several of the nuns died of the same thing, which laid 30 of them in their beds at once. She starts on Sunday evening for Roehampton, but does not know how long she will be kept there. ……………..

Convent of the Sacred Heart
121 Hammersmith Road
London W6

Dotty beloved

Will you write to me! You owe me one so you have NO excuse. To think that I have first got all your news from Connie.

Aren't you wicked?   Aren't you horrid?

I hear you have "Tabby Clayton" with you at Barra. Is it true? Kindly sit down and make me a picture of him in word or in sketch. His name is decorative!

Not quite certain what this creature is - but it is me feeling distressed. Yes I think that must be the reason.

Distressed because you have faded away

into a kind of ghost. I myself am just going to fade away into retreat

so can't be sure that I shall finish.

The Society of the Sacred Heart

The Society of the Sacred Heart was established in France by St Madeleine Sophie Barat in 1800, following the French Revolution, to provide educational opportunities for girls. The first school opened in Amiens in 1801, and in some cities there were at least two schools, a boarding school and also a day school for poorer children.

There were schools established in Australia, New Zealand and Africa, and in 1818 the first of many institutions was opened in America.

The French Government forced the closure of 47 of the Society's schools in the early part of the 20th century, and the motherhouse relocated in Belgium.

In 1842 the Society established a school/community at Berrymead (Acton). In 1850 it moved to Elm Grove in Roehampton.

In 1920 Lettie returned to Roehampton England where she taught until 1924. She was then transferred to West Hill, Wandsworth as Mistress General of the day school. Her years there were most fruitful. She was very skilful at helping families in need, and always most discreetly. It would be hard to number those who owed much to her.

It must have been while on leave from Calcutta in 1924 that Susan Burnett's parents took her to see her Aunt Lettie. "I remember being taken into a sort of pantry which seemed to a small child to be filled with shelves and shelves of square tins out of one tin she gave me some quite the most delicious biscuits I had ever tasted!

After a walk round the garden, I pointed to the oval-shaped lawn and remarked that I supposed that was her racecourse"

"Of course," said Lettie.

On one occasion one of her brothers called at Roehampton and asked to see her, only to be told she was in Retreat. "What!" he exclaimed, "Burnett in retreat?....Never!"

At the outbreak of World War II the Convent was moved from Roehampton to Newquay, and later to Stanford Hall near Rugby. In memory of Lettie, Worm's Eye View, which concludes this book, gives us further insight into Lettie's mind.

Mother Burnett's letters to Major and Mrs Dunlop are fascinating to read. Dorothy and Alexander Dunlop were the parents of Mary and Ann, pupils at Roehampton Convent. Alice Shields is the daughter of Mary who married Jack Michell in 1943.

From these letters, we get an insight into her duties as headmistress. She was responsible for the welfare of every single girl in the school, and her concern for Mary and Ann Dunlop's safety is clear in every line.

The letters also demonstrate how very difficult it was to communicate with parents serving in the army in far-flung corners of the Empire. What a sacrifice those parents made in living so far away and sending their children back to Britain for their education. One of the reasons Mary and Ann were sent home to school was for the good of their health. There was a constant danger of diseases such as cholera and rabies in India, so it was ironic that Mary became so seriously ill with scarlet fever at Roehampton.

Their parents came home to England each summer for the school holidays. This was an improvement from the generation before, when children were sent back to Britain to go to school and did not see their parents again until they were twenty-one. Mary and Ann spent their Christmas and Easter holidays with the Garnett family. Miss Rebekah Garnett is mentioned in one of the letters and had been the children's governess in India before they went to Roehampton.

After hearing of Mary and Ann's scarlet fever, their mother, Dorothy, set sail for England as soon as possible, finishing the last leg of the journey by aeroplane. It was the first time she flew.

Alice Shields writes. "Mother Burnett had a huge influence on my mother. Mummy admired and loved her, and we were brought up with many stories about MB. Mother Burnett clearly loved a joke. Once, when the school was celebrating a special feast day and there were no lessons, MB told the girls that she was going to hide, and they had to find her. The girls searched high and low but could not find her and had to give up. MB had hidden in plain sight and was walking in the garden reading her breviary and wearing the white veil of a novice instead of her usual black one."

Students with Lettie

Signed. Charlotte, Antonio, Marie Adelaide, Elizabeth, Termingarol

The letters that follow are those from Lettie to the parents of Ann and Mary Dunlop. These allow an understanding of the care that Lettie had for the children in her charge. When one thinks of her other responsibilities, and there is no reason to suspect that she did not treat all her girls similarly. One wonders how many head mistresses would take such trouble.

Convent of the Sacred Heart
Roehampton
London S.W.15

27 February 1935

My Dear Mrs Dunlop

Half term and all had been going splendidly as regards health when Mary complained on Monday (two days ago) morning of not feeling very well and as she had a slight throat, I sent her to the infirmary - a temperature of 100°. that evening, and Tuesday a rash all over, which the doctor says is Scarlet Fever.

Today Ann has come out exactly the same; she came up with a headache yesterday and exactly 20 hours after Mary, was covered with a rash and temperature 101°. We have had no illness in the school and neither Mary nor Ann have been to the parlour to see her friends nor out of the Convent since they got back! So where has it come from? One thing I was quite decided, was that the children should not go to hospital as the doctor of course wished, and they are both in our "Retreat House". You know the building beside the Great tree and the avenue down to the playing field. But I had to get a nursing Sister, (less expensive and much nicer than a lay nurse) to avoid infection. She will sleep down there next to them and there is a little kitchenette.

Both children normal and very well! Except for rash which I beg Ann not to scratch! I was down with them yesterday evening for an hour and will be able to go quite safely till they peel, when the troublesome time comes of dressing up for visits! Such a nice nursing Sister, they both like her. A Hope Sister.

Do not worry, only please pray that we have no more. I can not think how they got this germ and only thankful they are both so well.

Your letter earlier in the term saying that Mary's report was a disappointment would have been well made up for by her results of this half term. Her work has improved so much and she has been so good, just the dear child Mary can be at her best. Ann thinks this development a great treat as Mary is in the same boat!

I will write again in the next mail.

Yours as always in Christ.

L M Burnett rscj

The letters written after a Sacred Heart nun's name are r s c j Originally it meant: Religieuses du Sacré -Coeur de Jésus or Religiosae Sanctissimi Cordis Jesu.

20 March 1935

Dear Mr Thomas,

(Note. Mr Thomas must have been the member of the family to contact in an emergency. Mary and Ann Dunlop's parents only returned from India each summer holidays.)

I waited till after Mary had seen the specialist and the wire sent last night gave you the news. - This morning the doctor found her better.

You will have seen by my first letter that both children got Scarlet Fever three weeks ago. Where from I cannot say, for we had no illness in the school and they were never out anywhere except in the Convent Grounds. For the first 18 days all went not only well, but very well. Then on Friday the nurse was puzzled by her quick pulse. She had been below normal for 10 days so there was no reason for a rapid pulse.

The doctor saw her on Saturday and ordered her to be kept very quiet and lie flat. (She had not been allowed up, but was so well the doctor had promised she should, when the three weeks were up on Monday). On Sunday the pulse was still faster and on Monday nearly 130 so our doctor asked for a second opinion and the Children's doctor from Guys came yesterday evening. He told me the next few days were very important and asked for a special nurse for night duty, which I got. He says that it is the same poison that often attacks the heart after rheumatic fever, but that with careful nursing, he thinks all ought to go well.

I asked if I should wire her parents. He said no. He did not think that was any good in so doing, that it would only frighten them, that a letter by next mail explaining things is the wisest course. I think you will argue with this? I have of course written by the last two mails – I first missed the first one for Mary went to bed on a Sunday and I hope this week will bring her an answer from India.

It was not till Mary got your letter last week that I knew that you lived in Dublin. I shall send you word every day by PC and shall ring through if there is any change to frighten us. Ann is so far going on very well.

Believe me, with kindest regards

Sincerely yours in Christ

LM Burnett rscj

 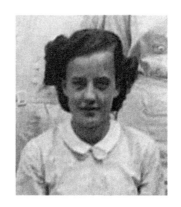

Mary and Ann were two of her pupils of whom Lettie was clearly very fond.

There is no reason to think that she was not just as caring to all of her girls many of whom came from far and wide.

They included three of the sisters of President Kennedy

(L) Zannick Hulton to whom there is reference in the letters below doubtless not least, Lettie's niece, Bridget Forbes Burnett (R)

22nd March 1935

Dear Major Dunlop,

I have had an anxious week since I last wrote, but D.G., I think Mary has turned the corner - And if you have no wire before this letter arrives all should be very well again. I will send a telegram in 10 days time from now, giving you news, for I know how anxious you will be after you receive this letter.

In my last to their mother, I think I asked if Mary's pulse was naturally a fast one? for on Friday evening (March 15th) it was a little rapid. On the 16th the doctor saw her and ordered her to be flat and rest instead of sitting up in bed as she had been doing. On Sunday, despite the rest the pulse grew still faster and on Monday morning it was nearly 130. The doctor asked for a second opinion and we got Dr Handsons the Child's Specialist from Guy's Hospital - after consultation they told me that the trouble was that the poison had gone to the heart and absolute quiet (not even feeding herself) so Ann was put in another room and I got a special nurse for Mary that evening.

A very full discharge from the left ear (without any pain and nothing to do with mastoid) gave an outlet to the poison and the pulse gradually slowed down to 100.

Today Friday

Dr Chambers was <u>very pleased</u> and says all now should go on well - but slowly and of course with great care. There has been no fever except a rise from below normal last Monday to 99.4. Temperature is again normal and pulse 100 and more steady. I thank God you have been spared these days of anxiety – The children's uncle, Mr Thomas, who rings up every day from Dublin is in touch with me and I was glad to be able to let him know what was being done. Mary is so good about keeping quiet and understanding.

The discharge from the ear is continuing and this I am told is good, till all the poison has drained away. She is not in any pain, nor of course does she know how very ill she has been this last week – In these days she was very weary. Now today and yesterday she would like to talk more than is good for her if allowed.

Little Ann, Thank God, is well but has not been allowed up. The doctor thought it wisest to keep them in bed for the full four weeks and has turned out to be right. Ann is in the next room to Mary with a little friend Lucy who had a light attack, and this keeps Ann from feeling lonely.

Now please remember that this letter will be followed up by a wire on the 3rd of April. If you have not heard before then, it is all good news, and my wire will be only a confirmation of this.

You will of course hear again by next mail. I have told both children that I am writing instead of them and they both send a great deal of love and "hope that Mummy will be home soon."

Of course, as Mary would not be fit to go away even at the soonest for some time, I will keep Ann here as well till you arrange what you would like best and have written to tell Mrs Garnett not to expect them these holidays.

With my kindest regards and full understanding of what it must mean for you and their mother to be so far from the children at such moments.

I am in Christ, very sincerely yours

L.M.Burnett rsj

16 Jan 1936

My dear Mrs Dunlop

The children both returned having I think enjoyed the holidays. Mary seems thinner than when she left but otherwise perfectly well. D.G. The end of last term was most satisfactory and of course Mary was delighted beyond words at the result of the consultation! What we had said all along about the quick pulse was evidently right but it was more satisfactory to get the specialist's verdict.

Now this term I thought with Mother Ponsonby that, unless there was something very special that Mary wanted to do, she had better go on with her rest after lunch for 3/4 of an hour - and of course no games, but dancing in the evening the doctor said was perfectly safe.

Since I began this letter, Mary has paid me a visit to tell me all about the holidays. She loved everything and everybody in the big family.

Both she and Ann were disappointed at not having the private room again, but I could not spare it as it was no longer really necessary and have given Mary the large cubicle in the junior school so she can have "Second Rising" every day except twice. This I think she probably still needs – Ann is in the next cubicle, so Good-nights can be said!!

About lessons - Mary has begged to give up Latin and Mother Shepherd thinks that, as she is now having extra French, this could be allowed without loss as Mary finds great difficulty over languages and probably would never make much of the Latin. I take it you have no objection?

I hope <u>you</u> are well yourself. You have to make up for the last six months my dear!

With love from yours affectionately in Christ

LM Burnett rscj

April 1937

My dear Dorothy

(Note. MB began addressing Mary and Ann's mother as Dorothy, not Mrs Dunlop as before. They had become closer and less formal over the two years, perhaps due to the children's illness.)

I must enclose this card. It will please you as much as it did me! The children are delighted about the Coronation. They have been granted 3 seats not 4 but one could hardly have expected that. I wrote as your husband directed and sent cheque. They refunded me the 15 / - as you see by enclosed which I send as it seems it must be signed. Zannick is in Rome and will be late back (the day <u>after</u> the procession) so that saves a disappointment.

I will be seeing the children on Tuesday but want to get this off before school reopens when I shall be swamped!

<u>Soon</u> <u>you</u> will be back and I join with you in looking forward to the joy of the long Summer holidays. Isn't it lovely to look forward to. Mary doesn't know yet but I am going to take her for the chief part in the Play we are going to do for Prizes "Saul" by Browning. Mary will be David and I think will be perfect if does not get frightened of it. - - She will learn her part with me!

Always much love my dear

from yours in Christ LM Burnett rscj

Kindest regards to your husband <u>of course</u>! pray God will keep him safe.

98

A very happy New Year!

Your letter, my dear, has just arrived and I am so glad you have got hold of a room, or rather that Pat has - for Ann

The "Kitchens" were full up so are we and I had got no nearer finding anything and was about to suggest the Anglican Convent !!!

Your Ann is a darling and I hope she and Pat will make the way over to Stanford sometime before Easter. I am counting upon Ann to keep us in 'Touch'!

I couldn't bear to lose my Dunlops after all these years –

As always in Christ with love from LM Burnett rscj

Stanford Hall

The school was evacuated during the war. They settled at Stanford Hall. Eventually the school moved to Woldingham. Roehampton took a direct hit in the bombing and the chapel was destroyed.

Stanford Hall by Sister Catherine Blood

Convent of the Sacred Heart
Stanford Hall
Rugby

Aug 17th 1943

My dear Mary

I have been slow in answering and returning the Red Cross forms. It was very good of you to send them and I hope poor Zannick (Hulton) will now get our letters. Who would ever have thought that she would be the one to go through so much suffering and sorrow.

Rosemary Hulton wrote only once – now over a year ago when I first got on to her to find out if she corresponded with Zannick. When shall we see you again - or Ann now that she is going to join a particular Service! Do you see whose writing is on the envelope? Mother McConachie's who sends very much love to you both. She has addressed to your letter to Donhead. I suppose you were only taking 24 hours off when you wrote to me - What about a certain naval officer? I hope all goes well with him.

Have you heard that Martine is engaged but it is supposed to be a Great Secret! Only as every school friend knows it, I don't think I am being indiscreet!

I hope that Ann will manage to stop off at Rugby if she has to come past that station. We expected a visit from Pat Tew and herself - but Alas ! it never came off.

Tell Ann that the Old Brigade have left and only Monique Vinci and Roz remain to put weight into the Firsts! The former will now be head of the school after eleven years. Hard to beat.

Please give Mummy my love. Someday I hope we shall all meet at a restored Roehampton

With much love. Always affectionately in Christ

LM Burnett rscj

Note

MB kept up a correspondence with her girls and was well informed about their engagements and marriages. A few weeks after this letter, Mary Dunlop became engaged to the 'certain naval officer,' Jack Michell and they were married on October 5th 1943 at St James Church, Spanish Place. Pat Tew was the younger sister of Mary Tew who went up to Oxford to read anthropology. The school had a whole holiday (a day off lessons) when Mary got her place. It was a huge achievement to get one of her girls into Oxford. Mary Tew's married name was Douglas. Mary Douglas became a professor of anthropology.

From 1931 to 1939 Lettie was back at the Roehampton Convent and was evacuated with them to Stanford Hall during the war.

As Mistress General she was always ready to take a class if a nun fell ill, and no matter what the class was meant to be, it was always Scottish History if given by Mother Burnett, and very racy history at that!

Stanford Class by Sister Catherine Blood

Mother Burnett's Room

The world is wide, the hills are high, the rivers deep and clear,

So many things to think about, so much to see and hear

But write I not of dream-known lands, where flowers ever bloom

The sacred place I dare to praise, is Mother Burnett's Room

For up the marble staircase, from the corridor below

Or down the darkened passage, to the wooden door we know,

Study-room and classroom, whether morning, night or noon,

Every road appears to lead to Mother Burnett's Room

Often comes the doubtful one, with talk of dire need,

Asks advice, or makes excuse, or tells of worthy deed

The Saint awaits his glory, and the sinner meets his doom

There's much to do and more to say, in Mother Burnett's Room

So many things of interest, and secrets yet untold,

Puzzle both the mistress and the little six-year-old,

For, behind the wooden door, far from fear and gloom

There the school is organised, in Mother Burnett's Room

The world is wide the hills are high, the rivers deep and cool,

And tho the world is mighty, why the world is but a school

The Saint is given glory, and the sinner meets his doom,

Within the place that to the world, is Mother Burnett's room.

And so, when I am older, if the world is seldom kind,

If I know not what to do, nor where advice to find,

The memory of childhood, when the night is filled with gloom,

Will take me up the marble stair, to Mother Burnett's room.

Moira Hayes. aged 15

Latter days

After the War, when her heart was beginning to fail and she had to lead a very quiet life, Lettie spent her time making lovely toys and painting on silk. In 1945 she went back to West Hill and did private work at the Froebel College. Later at Hammersmith, when her memory began to fail, she would still see hundreds of old friends annually until the queue had to be controlled. She was indeed a wonderful mixture and to many, the greatest friend of their lives.

1951 saw her at the Hammersmith Convent where she spent the last fifteen years of her life. Her health was ailing and her memory was playing tricks and she lived more and more in the past.

Lettie's memoirs end on a note so typical of her.

'And the last phase is Hammersmith, now nearing its end for I write in 1960. It is not possible for me to find words full enough of gratitude for all I owe the dear Society - for the patience of my Sisters and the kindness and love of my Superiors. Only the Lord can repay, and with all my heart I ask Him to do so - heaped up and flowing over of His own precious consolations on those who have been so kind to me and mine.'

Lettie and Dorothy

As she grew weaker and her mind became more muddled, one wish was foremost - to return to her beloved Scotland. This, with the help of her sister, Dorothy Irvine, she was able to do.

Postcard to Dorothy

SCJM. — Convent Sacred Heart
Hammersmith W.6.

Greetings
& best wishes
for 1964.
Send me news
of yourself &
don't forget you
have an aged
sister !! Send
my best wishes
to all, for a very happy
New Year ——
L.B.

Mrs Irvine
Barra Castle
Old Meldrum
Aberdeenshire .

P.S.S.
as this must go into an envelope!!
add more love & more good wishes!
hope you are quite WELL ?

She was visited by the nuns from the Aberdeen Convent and on one occasion by one of her "old girls", then Vicar of the Irish viciarate, who wrote "Age had settled down on her ardent spirit, but the eyes still twinkled with humour and affection. She did not remember me as the 'old child' she had taught, but she recognised me for what I represented, the Society which she loved. That little visit did me much good. I found in her a tranquil spirit, content with God's Holy Will. When I renewed my vows with her, I was conscious of the fervour of her union with my prayers. May she now rest in Eternal Peace."

Lettie died in a home near Aberdeen in 1966.

In Memoriam

Worm's Eye View

"M.B."! Initials which can never fail to elicit a sharp response in the hearts of those raised by the bearer of that well remembered nickname. My own first reaction is the shiver of apprehension once felt in the blackboard jungle at the first sound of the prowling Mistress General - the second still being the instinct to desist from whatever I am doing.

Such was life at Stanford Hall. There was the unmistakeable rattle of a rosary in the basement corridors which drove any loafers in the far away attics scuttling like a lot of rabbits to the nearest refuge. Again, that handclap of hers, reverberating across the midland ridge and furrow, by which any pretended fugitive from M.B.'s reign of terror would at once be brought to heel ..... Then, too, her deep roar, often embellished by an imperious gesture from the unmistakeable short, thickset figure down by the glassy lake. Heart in mouth, the hearer's only recollected fault that of being anywhere in the facility, the victim would run helter-skelter as though in answer to the highest call of duty, scarce able, on arrival, to perform the perfunctory curtsey custom demanded.

From house-to-house and mouth-to-mouth in that conservative community deep in the heart of England, the buzz went round. There was to be a Nunnery next door! A Roman Convent had come and run up its standard in the land of two predominant passions - a lot of sport and a mistrust of "abroad". No good could come of it.

But as time will tell we had our saving grace. We had M.B. In full view of the wary world, nearly all day and every day, her black robed figure was to be seen fishing by the lake, assisted every now and then by a colt-like child's nimble fingers, recruited to disentangle the line from the blown veil in which it had got caught up. It was a never to be forgotten sight, well in the local tradition.

Heads began to nod, and when at last the Meet itself was invited to Stamford Hall and Master and Whips set off in proper form from the gravel in front of the school, M.B.'s public acceptance was complete.

That was all there was to it. M.B. had passed common entrance and so, by association, had we. From then on it was only "O.D.T.A.A." she confessed, she laid her finger along her nose in order to hide her amusement and delight at being thus conversant with the local jargon. In "one damn thing after another", M.B. listened to and commiserated with the landlords on their roofing problems, their heating problems, the staffing problems and indeed all the problems of estate management inside and out. The Three R's were all right in their place, but there was a war on and, having won her first battle, M.B. now had had no hesitation in setting the slave labour at her disposal to the task of digging in. We soon learnt the cost of keeping up the stately homes of England, but by and by, as we weeded the endless drives, we found our roots taking hold through the uncharitable soil on which we worked.

Thus in default of all the equipment proper to school not excluding books, M.B. seemed resolved that we should get our culture in the liberal traditional appropriate to our Georgian setting. She was a terror but a holy one. Suddenly a child would find herself favoured by an invitation – one of many it would prove to be – to her eyrie in the library where, as one entered, M.B.'s person was hardly to be distinguished from the study chair before the fire.

Lapped in the sudden silence of book-lined walls, one was soothed by that evocative, mellow tang of a hunting squirearchy, so alien to a Convent, yet so harmonious with Mother Burnett's personality.

Together we would browse through something we had somehow together selected, and together fall under the spell of an absent Englishman's taste in ageing prints of flowers and birds, or fish and flies, not to say a private collection or two of letters from literary relations long since dead. In this way we were taught to dip, dive and swoop through the pages of English literature, lore and history. Nor was this new territory that we were discovering, but rather the old - the Old-Englishness of England.

So with lots of stick and some carrot, were we coerced, encouraged and eventually enticed to discover ourselves. Nor were we allowed to forget the drama through which we were then living.

Every day during lunch M.B. would read out long bulletins on the war. She would fix her gold spectacles on her not inconsiderable nose beneath those sandy brows and proceed to bring the events piling up around us vividly to life. Accordingly we judge the war by M.B.'s reactions to it. A trumpet blast on her handkerchief presaged a disaster to a beloved navy, and as she read, she would shake her paper into the light – perhaps the better to see but often just to gain time – and because she was one of those who regard the best thing in England as the high road to Scotland, she swelled with pride as she read the account of the Highland Brigade, with kilts swaying and pipes playing, marching, not indeed to victory, but into an honourable captivity at St Valery. M.B. in short, was our very own Churchill. It never crossed her mind either that England might fall to the enemy and we never thought of such a thing.

Her philosophy was not very obtuse. Life is to be lived on its own terms - we had to learn to live in the world as we found it. There was little room for reformers.

Thus, when previously we arrived at Newquay and M.B. saw what it would be to run a school under such conditions, there too she tempered the wind to the shorn lamb with all her wonderful genius for improvisation. With a blessing and a twinkle in her shrewd blue eyes, she sent us off, day after unbelievable day all through the first winter of the war, to paddle at Lusty Glaze

Small wonder, then, at Stanford, the county sent his daughters to her in an ever-increasing flood. She was "one of us" and in particular she never allowed any religious pressure to be brought to bear on her invaders, nor did she single them out in any way. Thus where she might have found hostility, there did she leave trust. For since she really pressed for an advocacy and never pointed a moral, M.B.'s lessons were non - lessons – often alas to be learnt the hard way. Nor was she shaken by disappointments. Necessity for learning them would be evident to her pupils in the end, if only many years after they thought that they had thrown off her yoke.

Our Mistress General knew the world and understood what each child needed to compete with it. She gave everything she had. Like it or not, once one had been under M.B., one would never again be quite free of her.

M Don January 1966

Postscript

When Lettie became a Roman Catholic at the age of twenty-three, she had no Roman Catholic relations. She liked to remember that her father, at the same age, had also wanted to become a Roman Catholic, but his parents in law refused to let their daughter marry a Catholic and so he could not convert. It was only on his deathbed, at the age of eighty, that he was received into the Church. It is ironic that – all those years earlier – he was the one who would have understood.

Printed in Great Britain
by Amazon

77647090R00071